# WHO YOU TRULY ARE

A collection of sayings and poetic rhymes that are gentle reminders of ***Who You Truly Are*** and pointers of how to return home when you get lost.

## TITLES

Stop Trying.......7
Know Who You Are.......13
Discover Your True Self.......17
Reflect.......23
This Very Moment Is Yours.......25
The Joy of Just Doing.......27
A Drop.......33
Rise.......35
The Journey to Your Sacred Centre.......39
It Is Time.......43
The Sacred Unknown.......45
Abide In Our True Nature.......47
You Are.......49
Your Journey, No One Else's.......51
Why?.......53
The Power of Thought.......55
Your Story Engraved.......59
Keep Shining.......61
Your Reflection.......63
Paint Your Beauty.......67
Be Your True Light.......69
A Call to Return.......71
The Call.......73
You Are Enough.......75
Different, But The Same.......77
Beauty in Vulnerability.......79
Image and Likeness.......83
Sembah Your Sacred Self.......87
Being You.......89
Light of This World.......91

## STOP TRYING

What are you trying to be or become?

Who are you trying to be?

And who is this "I" that you are trying to become or be?

Are they really you?

Is it even real?

Is it worth it?

STOP!

Quit leaving this moment.

Why?

Because you are enough, so please stop!

Trying? No need to try to become anything, you are exactly who you are, what you are, and it is totally enough, it is perfectly complete, so stop looking outside of this.

To be? No need to be anything, because you are a being, you are IT! It is you.

Trying to be means you are divorcing and abandoning yourself, your **true** Self and thus, stepping out of the moment.

This moment and your being are interwoven, interconnected without you having to do anything. So therefore, *you* are not required.

Why?

It's already happened.

Every single bit of you. And *you* had nothing to do with it. None of *your* effort was required.

It all happened through Cosmic Intelligence.

It is none of *your* doing.

You may say, "yes but..."

No buts!!

*You* had nothing to do with that process other than be.

So, quit. Stop. Give it up. Let go.

Can't you see that by trying, you are trying to become someone else other than what already is you?

Fundamentally, you are rejecting your true Self, and in doing so, you abandon the moment and therefore, you abandon life.

Why?

Because life is happening now and so are you!

Quit it. Stop. Return immediately to "I am enough" and "this moment is enough".

Now. Always, and forever.

No need to look outside of yourself, or try to become someone or something else.

You are perfectly and wonderfully made. Everything you are is enough.

This always was, and forever will be. No need to search for more, fight for more, struggle with or try to enforce. The work is complete.

How?

Because you are already complete.

You are completely, wholly enough with nothing more to be added or taken away.

Just accept and allow you to be. It is enough and start to experience your ***enough-ness!***

Otherwise you will never experience your true, authentic and real presence.

Your presence is a beautiful thing, something that is a gift to all of us.

Your very presence is everything.

It is the sunshine, the rain, the wind, the stars, the smile, the tears, the joy, the sadness, the loss, the hug, the dance, the stillness.

It is all in your enoughness, in this very moment, expressing and united with all eternity.

## KNOW WHO YOU ARE

Have you ever thought how amazing your life would
be if you discovered who you are?
To begin with, know that you are set apart.
You are a very distinct, unique, independent
individual. And for that reason alone, you must
celebrate and honour your coming.

Your coming here was no mistake.
You are here to live your full,
authentic true existence.
Not to copy the crowd but to tap into your true spark,
your essence, your very real presence.

You are a very exceptional being.
It is only that you might not be seeing.
A blur in your vision,
a darkened view,
you might not be perceiving or simply believing.

You are complete.
Full.
Whole.
Thoroughly intact and that's a fact!

Don't let others impart their own crazy ideas of who
they think you are, when they don't even know
themselves, just to tear you apart.
No, no, no!
Protect your heart, your life, and place a circle around
it. Remember you are set apart only so that you can
experience your true life, a higher calling.
So, be brave and start walking,
take strides and create the right vibes.

You are a living being, awoken, breathing, conscious, a spark of energy that carries the eternal DNA of the entire universe.

You are not this weak piece of existence that is here to be messed around with. You are a star, a light, a creative flow of energy that has the capacity to think, create, imagine, envision, devise, depict, perceive, realize, and invent the most majestic, ***out of this world*** plan, or outline for your life. This is one of your internal powers that you must not waste.

A certain Guru once told me, "Steve, you must learn to work with your inner paint brush and paint the life that you feel inside that you know is for you."

Don't wait for others to interfere with your paintwork. Get busy painting, crafting, shaping and forming your artwork. Your spirit is greater than any fear, than any obstacle, than any hurdle, than any bump or hardship that you may face here on Earth.

Spirit is always greater than matter, but you have to know this. Everything you see on the outside was first born from the inside.

So, rise up and walk your victory.
Rise up and walk your destiny.
Rise up and walk your future.

Through the realm of the unknown and by faith, courage and the conviction, know that greater is your light than anything you may face.

Are you listening to my spirit speaking to yours?

## DISCOVER YOUR TRUE SELF

What is your true nature like?
At essence, it is pure presence.
It is an energy that always was.
It is forever eternal.
It knows no death, neither can it be destroyed,
or for sure remain void.

It has an image,
but if misdirected,
it can be deeply affected,
wrongly connected,
seriously infected.

This image has a potential lightness,
an immense brightness,
but only if you walk in its likeness.
So please be a correct witness,
or you may end up with some sickness.
A distorted, polluted, image or outline is like
having too much drink.
You cannot think,
you'll stink,
be on the brink,
and then need a shrink!

To know the inside, you have to travel in,
this is where you have to begin.
Travel deeper than the skin,
until you see your very twin.

To know thyself,
is the greatest of all wealth.

You may ask, "what might I discover underneath this cover?"
A lover?
Or joy that I once knew as a boy?

It is peace that melts all the pain,
all the shame,
so that you can regain!

Kindness that removes all blindness.
Goodness that is deeply rooted in wholeness.
Faithfulness which leads to gratefulness.
A gentle softness which heals all broken-ness.
Self-control to handle any burning candle,
real wisdom to pass through the system,
real knowledge from the inner college,
or faith, the very substance of the unseen,
the invisible into the visible.
The power to recover and renew,
to dissolve every type of flu!
To heal and kill all the unwanted chills.

The ability to speak and make things happen,
with words that bring life,
carry power,
life giving,
deeply forgiving.

The intuition to know what is right, with no fright.
No tension, I have to mention,
but a yielded trust with no rust!

Discerning the moment, this very hour,
intuitive knowing, the all flowing, it's showing!

To converse with Angels, and an Avatar,
with the beautiful Stars from afar.

But this potential is only realised, discovered or
found, once you really touch the ground!

## REFLECT

Have you ever wondered about your life?

What are the thoughts, or the emotions, the words, the actions, the deeds, or activities that allow your spark of light to brighten?

Your lamp to lighten, your spark to sparkle.

What are the things in your life that fill your heart with rays of warmth, of love, of gratitude?

What are the moments that you have observed that have truly brightened and filled your heart with awesomeness?

With an overwhelming sense of deep appreciation for what life has given you.

Sometimes, observing these moments are the biggest clue to our peace, to our happiness, to our purpose, and are the real sign-posts that we need to observe.

But maybe you have stopped following these wonderful clues or signs because they are pointing to a different way, another expression of life than the one you see the majority are living.

But hand on my heart dear friend, dear brother, dear sister, these signs are like angels pointing you home, pointing you to a place of safety, pointing you back to your light. These moments are also like the oil that will keep your fire burning, and your love strong, your compassion overflowing, and your actions charged with kindness.

## THIS VERY MOMENT IS YOURS

This very moment you're in, is meant to be what it is. It may be painfully lonely, or too emotionally demanding, slightly confusing, even unrecognisable.

Absolutely not matching up with anything you have been taught, believed, expected, or at all wanted. And the sense of "I don't want this" or "please just go away" or "when is it all going to change?" is pressing on you.

How do you know that this very moment that you are wrestling with or resisting is the very moment that is required to propel you into a new way of life?

You see, my good friend, it is not an accident. You are not an accident. This very moment that you're experiencing has a deeper calling. And the pain or anguish that you are feeling is only your resistance to it.

New wine demands new wineskin.
A new approach. A different response.
A new attitude, and nothing to be afraid of.

The very thing you thought was potentially killing you is the very thing that is going to make you!
So now you can approach this moment with a wild embrace, an open heart, with invitation and a deep sense of gratitude. This moment is your special moment.

It is your sacred, unique experience, becoming part of the many pages in your life's diary.

## THE JOY OF JUST DOING

Nowadays, people only want results, but this only leads to insults, competition, and the sense of feeling happy only when something has been accomplished.

If you raise your kids on success alone and not their efforts they will grow to feel that they are never enough, always looking for the next, never feeling content with the joy of their efforts, or ever enjoying the process of doing it for the love of it.

The love of anything ***is*** the reward. If you love martial arts, dance, or artwork, the love of doing it ***is*** your reward.

And if, by magic, you are able to make a living out of it, well that's a huge bonus.

But never forget the love of doing ***is*** the reward.

This way, you will always do the things you love. Most kids love doing something, whether it's maths, science, sports, art or music, and are totally happy with just doing.

But the moment they are pushed into doing it for success, or for it to become their livelihood, they normally quit.

Why?

Because they enter the realm of competition, doing it to win, to gain, to succeed.

The love they once enjoyed is drained by the stress and anxiety of achieving and winning.

And when it doesn't happen in the way society measures success, they normally quit, or most certainly lose the joy of the experience.

This is very sad because life gifted them with a love, a passion. And having something you love to do is very important for one's internal health. There is a lot of suffering in life so having something you love to do is also a safe refuge.

This is the Law of Love.

Once applied, it keeps you in union with everything. Avoid the stress of becoming anything, but rather, reside in love.

So please, don't throw things you love away because you haven't made money out of them, or they don't match up with people's expectations of "success".

Please don't quit doing them because life is very short and having this love is a wonderful treasure.

Never quit them.

Let go of what you think they can give you, because what they have given you already, the joy of doing it - is your reward!

It's your beautiful personal treasure that life has shared with you, and enjoying them is a wonderful gift to you.

The joy is your reward, that very deep emotion that gets you up looking forward to doing it, is a reward in itself.

You had that once, and you can return to it.

Please don't say it's too late, or you're too old, or you can't. Because you can, it's a choice my friend, a choice you can make today.

And the moment you do, it will open up parts of you that have been closed down or forced to shut down.

Your joy is your strength!

Remember when you were a young boy or a young girl? How you played, how you danced, how you sang freely, when you enjoyed reading this or that book, or the comics, the movies you watched, the fun of riding a bike or simply the joy of giggling and laughing?

There is no need to lose these simple joys, never!

## A DROP

You are just a wave in the ocean, a drop of water in the sea, a cloud in the sky, a blade of grass in a field, a ray of the sun.

But, you are very much part of the ***whole***.

It is you and you are it.

In this, you are not required!

You were never required and won't be required.

You had nothing to do with it.

So just allow things to be.

We call this principle ***Zero (0) interference***.

Allowing life to be and change from one form to the next, knowing that it is woven together in a life tapestry serving the All, always.

No need to interfere.

You are enough!

## RISE

So, they tried call you names that have stained, they tried to frame but it was all in vain.
You rose above the pain, and now who's in shame?

But wait a minute, that was only their opinion, normally infected because deep drown they felt rejected, and so what they projected was a soul that was deeply dejected!

Your real name doesn't know shame,
your true essence, is connected to your real presence.

So don't bow to their vow,
you just keep following the Tao!

You true nature lies at the core of who you are, "come on now, it's time to raise the bar, inject some new fuel into that car"

Okay, so sometimes it gets buried, or even lost but for a little cost.

But if you're willing to dig, invest and look deeply into your chest, you will hear its gentle whisper breathing new life.

"Time to rise, get up, move forward, hear your calling, no more stalling, you're done with crawling.
Rise, learn and be wise!"

Let go of the heavy, and move into the steady, like a tree rooted, able to withhold, time to be bold, enough with the fear, the secret tear.

Stop hiding, time you were gliding.

I've heard your noise, to be honest there just a bunch of excuses.

The real reason is you are scared to enter your correct season!

So, stop pointing the finger at others and look in the mirror, we all know deep down who really shivers.

Hiding behind your fake accounts that isn't you, that's not true.

We all know, we can feel your flow.

So, man up, turn up, so you can free up, instead of hiding because you're scared of get beat up!!

Hear me out, you need to spar, enter the circle, cripple your fears, go through your tears, slay your dragon!"

Come out of your den, shall I count to ten?

## THE JOURNEY TO YOUR SACRED CENTRE

There comes a point in your life when exploring the outside has to come to an end. And the most important journey of your life is about to begin: the journey into your ***Sacred Centre***.

This is the journey what ancient Masters called, ***"the journey from the head to the heart".*** I like to call it ***"internal journey home".*** I say "home" because this is your true abode.

The place where your deepest and most precious thoughts lay, but it can only be activated through stillness.

Quiet abiding.

The busy-ness of the mind is slowly put at ease when you put a full-stop to grasping, grabbing, pushing or striving.

All of these characteristics are but a mere sign that you haven't come home yet. Your home is calling you. The place of rest, restoration, renewal and true joy.

This place I call home is the real YOU.
It's the untarnished, unblemished, uncompromised, authentic point that the Ancients call your ***"centre".***
Few find it.
Few choose to trust it.
Few make their nest there.

But I am encouraging you, inspiring you and challenging you to direct all of your forces back home.

You can start today by simply sitting quietly, in a comfortable space and slowly start returning through quiet breathing to the Sacred Space.

Once you are there, you will know exactly what I am talking about ☺

## IT IS TIME

When something is pulling you down,
preventing you from moving forward,
or simply wasting your time.
It's time to let it go!

So, put it down, take some steps to move forward and never pick it up again.
The quicker you do this the better.

Soon you will feel the release you deserve and the energy you were lacking will return.
It sounds easy right? It is!

So that thing that is preventing you from moving into your next page, your next chapter, stops you from fulfilling your destiny. It is but a choice away.

Make that courageous step today and spread your wings!

## THE SACRED UNKNOWN

There is a beautiful part of your life ahead that is full of mystery and a sacred unknown. We live in a time and culture where everyone wants to know what is ahead, what is in-between, below and above.

But life is unfolding unpredictable mystery, best left alone to flow and reveal itself. Allowing it to all happen. It reveals its true nature, trying to control its motions only lead to further struggle.

Remember when you were once that curious innocent child, living life, trusting the flow of time and space and allowing it to be what it is.
Until of course, we all got instructed to know everything, to manage everything, to control our lives rather than letting it be the gateless gate, the pathless path, the formless form.

And that is the real beauty of life. It is in moments of not knowing that we get surprised. It is in these moments spontaneous action is birthed, and we slowly return to home, to true authenticity.

Let go of the gate, the path, the tradition, the form and watch life flow.

## ABIDE IN OUR TRUE NATURE

Love is all around, in the food we eat, in the air we breathe, in the sun that shines on us, through the seasons, and yet we are unaware of it.
Why?
Because the *self* prevents us from feeling it.

That's why the self/ego is called a thief. It robs us from absorbing, knowing and experiencing this love that is all around. We fail to look deeply enough.

I know it is sometimes difficult to look beyond the veil of hurt, disappointment, fear, worry, pain, greed that are spinning and locked onto our ego and pain bodies. But Love is all around, everything is made of it, every cell of the body and the whole of creation is the result of Divine love.

"Beloved, let us love one another, for Love is the All and the All is Love, and everyone who loves is born of Love and knows Love."

*For the All is love and whosever abides in love abides in the All, and the All in him/her.*

This is our true nature, sadly lost at times when we allow ourselves to be consumed with the desires of the "me, myself and I".
*For unless the seed of the ego drops and dies, the true light of our nature will not shine its true image and essence.*

*For those who drop and dare to die will gain their true essence, and those who hold on and grip, to their false self, will lose their true nature.*

## YOU ARE

You are the stillness you seek.

You are the liberty you search for.

You are the moment that calls you.

You are the beauty you chase.

You are the peace you wrestle for.

You are the moment you ask to be in.

You are that presence, and it is you.

You are the practice you practice.

You are the life you search for.

You are light you switch on.

You are the truth you require.

You are the wisdom you grab.

You are it and it is you.

And so, the search ends and stillness, begins.

## YOUR JOURNEY, NO ONE ELSE'S

Don't let people tell you who you are, or what they think you are, how much strength you have or don't have, people don't know what you possess or have inside.

They don't know your journey, what you have endured, what you have suffered, the hours you have put in. Do not take other people's opinions too seriously. Keep listening the quiet vision you have in your heart and look to please no one!!

You are here to be contented and fulfilled and that will only happen when you follow the small whispers of your own unique individual heart!

The way you see things is deeply special. Different, but special! Do away with paying attention to those who are too afraid to follow their own.

## WHY?

Do you ever ask yourself these questions?

It's like having an internal session, in the spirit of stillness, and contemplation.

Why I am here, and why do I have these fears?

Was I born with them or were they learnt, copied, developed, transferred?

And what are my fears?

Are they habits, past memories, locked experiences, warped perceptions, or mere thoughts?

Who am I?

Does the "I" that I think I know really exist?

Am I a human being, or have I become a human doing, a program, a machine in a time-table?

Am I following the crowd, or following my fears, or am I being directed by my insecurities rather than my centre, my core, my deepest and truest conviction?

Do I treat myself with the love and respect I truly deserve?

What is one thing I could start doing today to improve the quality of my life?

When was the last time I told myself "I am enough."

When was the last time I heard the words "I truly love you."

Is there someone who has hurt or angered me that I am still carrying that hurt? Do I have to let go?

What does my presence really contain, do I transfer a peaceful life, one of love, joy, warmth, humility?

Honestly and truly, what do you transfer?

## THE POWER OF THOUGHT

We are what we think,
it happens in a blink.
Some thoughts can make you shrink,
even turn you to the brink.
Sometimes they even stink, don't you think?
With thoughts we form our inner.
So be aware, the thoughts that tare,
you should, my brother, care.
These things have power,
they form like a storm.
In the realm of the unseen,
they begin to take a hold,
until they fold,
causing you to hold,
removing your bold,
creating a heart that is cold.
If you allow this, it will mould.
Thoughts can turn to wild emotions,
like horses with wild forces,
running to and fro,
with nowhere to go.
Looking for a ride,
a wild tide.
A thought-form can be like a dragon,
a snake,
a lizard,
a cold blizzard,
an internal heat,
from your head to your feet.
A controlling force,
like that wild horse.
An addiction with immense friction,
An attachment that is bent on stealing your rent.

A grip that leads you on a wild trip,
Oh flip!!!

Here's a tip:
STOP!
Just stop until it flops,
like unfed crops,
or a balloon without air,
where is it going?
Nowhere!
Why?
It has no life.
No power.
No fuel.
It's lost its tools.
So, when you stop,
you pop,
you drop.
It rises,
you will see.
In due time, you kill the flee.
No force required.
Sit still.
You will.
Until.

## YOUR STORY ENGRAVED

Every line on your face tells a story of a life that has travelled through trials and tribulations, through loss and despair, through heartache and loneliness, through battles won and lost. And although people only see crooked deep lines of old age, these are the lines of your victory. They are the marks and true medals of honour. Ones that prove that you have never given up, no matter what you have faced!

Your face tells your story, the story that you are still standing through a long passage of time. The wrinkles are the proof of your bravery, the lines of your stamina, the marks of your character, they are the formations of your own unique life expression, and the signatures of your commitment to want to live a life that deeply challenges all of us!

There is no anti-wrinkle cream that can cover, or should, cover your medals of honour. Stand tall you older ones and know you have become more classic, like mature wine, you stand in the midst of us with deep wisdom and a knowing that is much needed at this time.

You are in a unique and privileged position.

Stand tall!

## KEEP SHINING

You are all incredible miracles of flowing creative energetic life, that has its own unique and brilliant expressions, opinions, views and aspirations waiting to flow out of you. Don't be afraid to express that. It is the very substance that makes you shine! It's your true light, so keep shining it!

You owe this to no one other than yourself.

To be honest, it's your true calling and gift to life. If it was shut down when you were a child, or lost, or even buried for a time, let today be the day you make a choice to let out, and value it! Even if no-one else does!

This has nothing to do with others, it is solely your business. So, don't expect people to understand it, like it, agree with it, or even encourage it!

It is your choice ok?!

But one thing I can tell you, when you do decide to make that choice, you won't be standing alone. Nature all around is pointing the same way, and you will feel yourself again, that's for sure!

## YOUR REFLECTION

What do you see and feel when you see your
reflection?
Your true light,
your true worth,
your oneness,
your beauty,
your journey,
your bravery,
your commitments,
your sacrifice,
your hard work?

Or have you forgotten?

If you have a moment today or tomorrow,
please take a deep breath and contemplate your life,
your journey, your precious moments.
And then take a breath in and bow to yourself with a
real sense of humility and respect.
It is important you see your life with worth and self-
recognition.

Why?
Because you are part of this ***sacred whole***,
you are a part of this ***cosmic whole***,
your existence is also important.
Your life is a deeply precious one,
your light also matters,
your smile also warms,
your hugs bring joy,
your existence has deep meaning and purpose.

Just maybe, you have forgotten it, that's all.
If you have, then dust the forgetfulness off and have a deep look at your precious life again.

Your light is closer than your breath.
You only have to become aware of it.

That's all.

## PAINT YOUR BEAUTY

Your ability to use your imagination and create a miracle is determined by many energetic forces working together.

Can you burst into a new vision of hope when the tide is going against you?

Can you rise above the clouds and see a beautiful sky when everyone is clouded with confusion?

Can you think outside the box and expand your awareness when everyone else is shrinking?

Do you have the courage and the confidence to trust what you really feel and see on the inside, even when your loved ones are telling you to throw the towel in?

Can you continue to persevere in that direction when you are not seeing the rewards you want?

Can you spend months or even years alone, when no one is around?

Vision, insight, imagination, faith, will power, courage, endurance, concentration, awareness, and above all, ***love***, they are all inner components that are required to work together if you are going to see your dreams and visions come to pass.

But in the process, please don't expect your friends to understand it.

Remember, it is ***your*** vision, it is ***your*** dream.

## BE YOUR TRUE LIGHT

Understanding your true essence has all to do with activating your presence.

Now, your presence, is always here and now,
wrapped in a beautiful crown,
not in some worried frown,
trapped in a mask that looks like a clown!

Your real groove has nothing to prove,
it does not need to show or earn its worth.

It is perfect as it is, it does not need more biz!

Your true nature, has nothing to do with "I hate ya!"

In its centre, it has no real pain, or shame, to be honest it more like a burning flame,

This flame has only diminished, but let me tell you that you are not finished!

It can awake, never break, then it's never too late, you can write your new fate!

Who you are is not a car, you're no machine,
you're a beautiful being, you're just not really seeing,
and this is the truth, I hope it's freeing!

Your real qualities are pure, in that I am sure!

## A CALL TO RETURN

When someone threatens the human existence and ignores the environmental laws that are here to protect us all, he harms the Earth, his own nature and our place of habitat.

When the planet partakes in such acts, the entire planet is under threat. And so, the Earth responds with great quakes. Fires spread like wild ghosts running to and fro, crippling entire forest lands. Tornados spin out of control, waters rise and fall causing huge floods, diseases spread, taking lives, young and old.

Death roams around without ever being a respecter of race, belief, age and creed. There will be no end until humanity lays down the weapons of mass destruction, returns with a humble heart and obeys the Universal Laws that are here to protect us all, and puts an end to this endless chase for money, power and possessions.

Woe to those at this time who are not hearing or seeing the signs of the times. Can you not hear our Mother travailing and calling you back to a life of simplicity? Can you not hear the signs that are increasingly becoming more destructive? Put an end to all the cruelty against all living creatures and obey the Law to Love!

## THE CALL

When the mountains call, when the forest whispers your name, when the rivers are inviting you to jump in, embrace the journey and travel lightly, slowly stepping and allowing your feet to kiss the Earth. May your journey be filled with mystery and marvel. May your heart re-awaken to inner the voice of the wind. May you be filled with lightness, slowly allowing the invisible currents of grace to lead you home.

If you can take a moment today and look up,
just look up at the awesomeness of everything,
and say to yourself, "WOW! I am part of all this miraculous, majestic, incredible mystery we call ***LIFE***."

Just for a moment, look up and feel deeply connected to the whole. Leave your worries aside, leave your past, leave your future, leave your cares, leave your disappointments and let downs and just feel part of the greater whole.
Why?
Because you are part of it.
That, up there, is also that is in you.
Stars shine, they sparkle, and so can you.
You are also meant to shine.
Remember when you had that sparkle in your eye?
Well, let the stars remind you today that it is time to sparkle again.

Let your light shine even brighter!

## YOU ARE ENOUGH

You are entirely, wholly, completely enough.

You have all the right stuff, you don't need to puff!

You are beautyfully and wonderfully handcrafted. How you look is your own special book. You don't need to change your face, just because you live in a space they don't agree with your race,

You are a unique combination, chemically, mentally, physically splendidly, one in a billion times, change to a trillion!

You are no mistake, a shamble, or some point in time that was a gamble.

There is a reason for your coming, it weren't only plumbing, it's not just the greats that pass through the gates.

You too have a reason, a purpose, a calling, stop stalling!

Observe for a sec, take a pause, a quick check!

## DIFFERENT, BUT THE SAME

Just because we are totally different doesn't mean you cannot love each other. Love is appreciating each other's differences, tolerating each other's mistakes and loving unconditionally.

We all need food, clothing and shelter, every bird needs a nest. I don't understand why humanity has to have destructive ideologies, or beliefs, when deep down we all require the same things, and everything has been prepared and provided for us beautifully.

We don't need *"ideas or beliefs"* when everything has been provided for us. I don't need an idea to pick an apple off a tree, or a mango, or a grape.

Everything has been provided. Humans only require an abode, a space, warm clothes, food and love for one another.

It is very simple.

## BEAUTY IN VULNERABILITY

To be a broken vessel,
from your continuous wrestle,
a tired soul,
a rejected foe,
whose lost the glow.

A broken heart,
all falling apart,
the sound of tears,
a mind full of fears,
and nothing seems clear.

And yet the moment is calling,
but you feel as though you're falling,
this is a warning,
so please here its calling!

It is gentle sound,
It is all around,
Its presence is near,
Its vision is clear,
Its waiting to wipe away your tear.

Its gentle whisper,
is like beautiful sister.

Its small still voice,
is calling you to trust and follow
for a new tomorrow.

To follow that voice,
is entirely your choice.

And if you do,
be sure that at your door,

there's a hand that always present,
in case you hit the floor.

So, if you open and trust,
let go and yield,
to this Presence,
this Light.
Let go of the fight!

Trust, it's your true light.

## IMAGE AND LIKENESS

You are a living being,
This is totally worth seeing,
Why?
Because it's freeing.
So don't turn yourself into a "doing", pursuing,
otherwise you might end up brewing.
Losing your true self,
ending up like an elf
on the shelf,
tired and wrongly wired,
with the sense that you were only hired.

You have the Breath of Life,
This in fact is your real *wife*,
Her name?
*Harmony*, she's wonderfully calm-*fully*,
if you listen to her carefully.
Her rhythm her rhyme is always on time.
It is in the moment, that she's in her prime.
You'll soon discover that she's so fine.

This life was given, so quit the driven,
this only leads to striven,
creating further tension,
closer to your pension,
I thought I would mention!

So, enter into grace and stop the chase,
end the race and experience your true face.

You are carrying the Image,

the exact inner mark, the real spark.
The one and only Presence,
the very real Essence,

of the Light and Sound,

never bound,
completely round,
yet always formless,
completely whole.
Your real nature,
it never hates ya!

And its purpose,
is for you to grow,
in the flow,
in this show,
so that you can glow,
deeply know!

Into its likeness,
it's very brightness,
to form a yoke,
this isn't a joke,
or a mixed-up Pope,
or cheap tasting coke.

This takes death,
encoded in your breath,
hear the call,
It's time to fall.

Enter the gate,
Your real fate,
Don't wait.

The Image has to become the Likeness,
the sign is the brightness,
the wholeness,
the boldness,
the power, the sound,
the might, no fright!

## SEMBAH YOUR SACRED SELF

Sembah or *"respect"* of thy Self is to truly recognize that you will never compromise your true light, your awareness, for money, fame, recognition, social respect for that sense of belonging.

When you are becoming so busy, so over-worked, so over-stressed, so downtrodden, so self-occupied that you no longer have time for ***you***, to listen to your precious heart, to go into your internal space, then you are already disrespecting your true Self.

It's honestly not worth it!

You are way too beautiful, too sacred, too special to sell your Self.

# BEING YOU

You have nothing to prove to anyone!
Only that you have done your very best.
Only ***you*** know when you have done that.

You know the strength of your spirit.
You know when it is time to say "Yes" or "No", so don't allow yourself to be put into situations where you can no longer feel your inner spirit.

For that is your most precious treasure and where your real strength lies. And it is in the unlocking of your inner strength that you will discover your power, joy, courage, compassion and peace.

Every day is another opportunity to rediscover something truly remarkable about who ***you*** are.

Your true essence, your true light, your true authentic you! For you have not been designed to be anything else but that. And remember, that is enough!

YOU are enough.

Start *NOW* by going *IN*.

## LIGHT OF THIS WORLD

You are the light of this world.
You are the light, yes YOU!
Just in case you say,
"me? Oh no, not me,
I'm just a little flee,
hiding behind the tree."

You are the lamp that can shine in any darkness,
that can heat any cold,
that can warm any heart,
that can point to the way,
that can help any astray.

You are the candle that sits on a table,
that can join two hearts
that have fallen apart,
that can sit in a home,
flickering its magic,
dissolving the tragic.

You are the torch that leads the way,
protecting those falling,
the lost, at all cost.
are you hearing its calling?
When you shine your light,
your love emanates,
it penetrates,
and creates
hope and healing.
The lost get found, like keys on the ground.

You are the light house,
that direct the ships,
from wild storms,
protecting lives,
from unseen waves,
and dangerous caves.
If only you knew its meaning,
your life would soon be beaming.
You are the light of this world,
so don't lower your worth,
or sell it over for a purse,
this only leads to a curse.

Your light is your essence,
Your most majestic presence.
It is the real you,
So shine, now is your time.
Let your power out without fear,
Be your true Self,
Don't hang it on the shelf.
Don't waste it or paste it on the wrong wall,
Please hear the call,
Stand tall.

You are a light,
Shining so bright,
Don't let this world prevent you from shining,
This is your moment,
Your experience.
So immerse,
Go deeper,
Climb steeper.
Your light is your real home,
You ain't no clone!

A light always reveals the way,
it opens the path and gives direction,
much more than just a projection.

Light is a sign of Life,
an indication that you are alive,
that you have energy,
that your batteries are on,
that life is moving.
So the question arises,
How does one keep this shining?
The sunflower reveals the key
For you and me.
Observe what it follows,
Today and tomorrow.
Observe its lines,
How it stands with its spine.
Observe its alignment,
Its concentration,
Its focus,
Its attention with zero tension.
Its only mission is its absolute vision,
to follows the light of the Sun…

Printed in Great Britain
by Amazon

69953606R00059